MEMORY PALACE

How To Remember Everything You Learn
A Guide To Learning With Unlimited Potential

Descrierea CIP a Bibliotecii Naționale a României
BROWN, ADAM
  MEMORY PALACE. How To Remember Everything You Learn. A Guide To Learning With Unlimited Potential / by Adam Brown. - București : My Ebook, 2018
    ISBN 978-606-983-598-2

159.9

MEMORY PALACE

How To Remember Everything You Learn

A Guide To Learning With Unlimited Potential

My Ebook Publishing House
Bucharest, 2018

CONTENTS

CHAPTER ONE: KNOWING HOW YOUR BRAIN WORKS 15

CHAPTER TWO: LONG TERM MEMORY 27

CHAPTER THREE: RESEARCHES AND FINDINGS ABOUT THE MEMORY 39

CHAPTER FOUR: MNEMONICS 45

CHAPTER FIVE: IMPROVING YOUR MEMORY: REMEMBER EVERYTHING AND ANYTHING 50

CHAPTER SIX: THE UNLIMITED POTENTIAL OF THE BRAIN 57

Conclusion 60

INTRODUCTION

I want to thank you and congratulate you for buying the book, **Memory Palace: How To Remember Everything You Learn; A Guide To Learning With Unlimited Potential.** This book contains proven steps and strategies on how to improve both your memory and the brain that made it possible to store information.

The book focuses on the power of the brain and its functions, especially the ability to store massive amounts of information, the various types of memory and how they all work.

As you read this book, you will also have the opportunity to learn how you can enhance your brain to take in more information and store them for a very long time and also the ability to retrieve the stored information no matter how long it has been stored.

As you know, forgetting things can be really frustrating and embarrassing. Imagine forgetting the birthday of your loved ones or your own wedding anniversary. What would happen if you forgot that your kid has a sports game or a play at school and you already promised to attend? Your kid would not be happy with you.

No matter how much stored information you are unable to retrieve, this book is sure to change all your frustrations and change your life forever. Imagine being able to remember anything you see, hear, smell, feel, and taste. Imagine the ability to keep the memories you don't wish to remember, perhaps because they are too embarrassing, traumatic or depressing and the ability to easily retrieve the happy events that have been stored in your memory.

This book is a sure bet to do all that. The first chapter of the book will take through the basics of the brain and how it works with the other parts of the body, how it sends information to and from the sense organs and stores information. You will also learn how to improve your brain operations, how to prevent forgetfulness and the exercises, strategies and foods that can improve your memory.

Once again, I congratulate you for purchasing this book. I hope you enjoy reading it as much as I enjoyed writing it.

Copyright 2018 by Zen Mastery - All rights reserved

This document is geared towards providing exact and reliable information in regards to the topic and issue covered. The publication is sold with the idea that the publisher is not required to render accounting, officially permitted, or otherwise, qualified services. If advice is necessary, legal or professional, a practiced individual in the profession should be ordered.

- From a Declaration of Principles which was accepted and approved equally by a Committee of the American Bar Association and a Committee of Publishers and Associations.

In no way is it legal to reproduce, duplicate, or transmit any part of this document in either electronic means or in printed format. Recording of this publication is strictly prohibited and any storage of this document is not allowed unless with written permission from the publisher. All rights reserved.

The information provided herein is stated to be truthful and consistent, in that any liability, in terms of inattention or otherwise, by any usage or abuse of any policies, processes, or directions contained within is the solitary and utter responsibility of the recipient reader. Under no circumstances will any legal responsibility or blame be held against the publisher for any reparation, damages, or monetary loss due to the information herein, either directly or indirectly.

Respective authors own all copyrights not held by the publisher.

The information herein is offered for informational purposes solely, and is universal as so. The presentation of the information is without contract or any type of guarantee assurance.

The trademarks that are used are without any consent, and the publication of the trademark is without permission or backing by the trademark owner. All trademarks and brands within this book are for clarifying purposes only and are the owned by the owners themselves, not affiliated with this document.

CHAPTER 1

KNOWING HOW YOUR BRAIN WORKS

The brain is one of the wonders of the world because of the so many amazing things it can do. It is arguably the most important part of the human body. It controls all the activities and operations of all the other organs in the human body. It receives information from the rest of the body, interprets the information and then guides the body on how to react.

The brain also helps with vital operations such as breathing, maintaining blood pressure and even releasing hormones. The parts of the brain include the cerebrum, the cerebellum, the brainstem and diencephalon. The technological devices we use today were all fashioned after the human body. Each device has the input devices, which can be compared to the hands, mouth, and nose on the human body.

The devices also have the output devices which can also be compared to the parts of the body that bring out waste products. Most importantly, the devices have the control section, which can be compared to the brain.

The part of the body we are interested in is the cerebrum. It is the largest part of the body and responsible for memory, speech, the senses, emotional response and so on. The brain works with all the five senses of the body and interprets all the information like odors, light, sounds and so on. The senses of the body include the eyes, the ears, the tongue, the nose and the skin.

The eyes provide sight, the ears provide a form of hearing, the tongue helps in tasting, the nose helps to smell, and the skin helps to feel things. Each sense organ has something called nerves which are directly linked to the brain. As a result, any information gained by each of these sense organs is transferred to the brain for interpretation.

The cerebrum is involved in reasoning, memory, planning and so on. When the eyes see anything, it sends the information to the brain which then saves it. The same thing happens to the other sensory organs. As an illustration, imagine a man who travels to another country, say Japan, and while there, he samples one of their delicacies. The taste of the food and its smell will be stored in the memory for a long time.

Now, imagine the man returning to his country. If he visits a restaurant and his nose perceives the smell of the food, the information will be sent to his brain and the memory will make him remember the name and smell of the food. The brain has very large storage capacity. As mentioned before, many of the storage devices of computerized devices were fashioned after the brain. We have the memory card, CD ROM, flash drive, hard disk and so on. All information is stored in these devices and can be retrieved anytime.

The same applies to the brain, whatever the eyes see, the nose perceives, the tongue tastes, the ears hear, and the skin feels are all stored in the brains and retrieved later.

There are two types of memory: the short term memory and the long term memory.

THE SHORT TERM MEMORY

For a memory to be created, information needs to be perceived first. When the information has been perceived briefly, it is then stored in the short term memory. The short term memory can keep very few items for few seconds. There are many ways to increase this and that will be discussed later as you read on.

It is also called the active memory and as its name implies, it keeps information for a very short period of time. One of the examples of things that can be stored in the short term memory is a phone number or number plate. The information in a short term memory can be reset by repeating the number to yourself. When information is important enough, the short term memory transfers it to the long term memory.

There are different ways by which information can be stored in the short term memory. One of these is by rehearsing. Rehearsing is an act of repeating something over and over again. For example, you see a car speeding away from the scene of a crime and you know that the police would need the information, so you quickly memorize it.

We can equate the short term memory as a generator which has a very small fuel tank such that if the fuel dries up and you don't replenish it quickly, the generator may go off. The same is applicable to the short term memory. The information is stored for a few seconds. If you don't repeat it and refresh it, you may never remember it again.

Another way by which information can be stored in the short term memory is when information is retrieved from the long term memory. When you are asked something that you already know and you needed to give out the information in a very short time, the information can be stored in the short term memory. An example is when you are asked the year you graduated from high school.

Information can also be stored in the short term memory the response selection and the selective attention. The response selection is a phase that occurs after a stimulus has been presented and before a response has been decided while selective attention can be defined as a process whereby one focuses on a particular object for a certain period. The latter helps to tune out details that are unimportant and focus on the important things.

There is a procedure that helps to measure how long a short term memory lasts and it is called the Peterson and Peterson procedure. The basic way it works is that rehearsal in the short term memory is not allowed to refresh information or transfer the information to the long term memory. The procedure then minimizes the rehearsal and ties up active processes.

SHORT TERM MEMORY LOSS

In this case, a person can remember events that happened many years ago but unable to remember what happened a few minutes earlier, like having trouble remembering what you just read or why you entered the kitchen. It is a very common problem. In this case, there are two types: the normal or mild forgetfulness and the serious type.

The mild forgetfulness could be not remembering something you just read, calling people you really know well by the wrong name, not being able to come up with the correct word, misplacing objects like your house keys or cell phone and so on.

However, when people begin to worry about your memory problems, that often show that your short term memory loss is serious. An example is when you keep asking the same questions, when you forget to eat when you don't remember your way home, when you forgot the content of a book you are reading. Many things can cause short term memory loss.

One of them is the lack of Vitamin B12. This deficiency can lead to so many confusions and dementia. Some medications like pain killers, sleeping pills and so on can also affect your memory. Other causes are too much stress, depression, and even anxiety. These three prevents you from functioning effectively.

Summarily, short term memory loss may often be a symptom of other medical conditions like Bipolar disorder, brain injuries, diabetes, epilepsy, schizophrenia, thyroid disorders and so on.

PREVENTING SHORT TERM MEMORY LOSS

To easily prevent something from happening, one has to know the root cause. Not having enough sleep is one of the causes of short term memory loss, then it stands to reason that a good night sleep will help to improve the short term memory loss. Therefore, to improve your brain, you need to get adequate sleep.

Another strategy is to find a way to reduce stress. Stress has been known to disrupt the brain's function. Therefore, you need to find a lot of ways to eradicate stress. One of these is by exercising, which gets your blood flowing freely. Other ways to reduce stress include mediation, decompressing, laughing out loud, and so on.

Avoid too much of processed foods which contain too much sugar. Too much sugar has been known to change brainwave patterns and cause insulin resistance in the brain. Unsteady supply of glucose leads to short term memory loss.

Smoking and heavy drinking also cause short term memory loss; you should avoid them.

CHAPTER 2

LONG TERM MEMORY

The Long term memory is a memory phase where information is stored permanently. It can also store virtually unlimited information for a very long time. Before information can be stored in the long term memory, it has to pass through the short term memory stage. When you can recall events that happened a few hours ago or many years ago, we refer to that memory as a long term memory. It stores information based on meaning, association, and importance. Some information in the long term memory is easy to access while others are not. You can easily remember information that is very important than that which is not.

For instance, you can easily remember events like your wedding day, the birth of your child, the day you graduated and so on simply because they are very much important. Easy recollection occurs when you reaccess a memory time and time.

Many things determine how long information can be held in the long term memory. One of these is the way the information was stored in the first place. Were you physically active and sober at that moment? Were you very alert and conscious? The information at that moment will remain vivid and last very long compared to when you were drowsy when the information was being stored.

People who study a lot will notice that repeating information over and over again while studying makes them recall in easily when they need it because such information often sticks around. The more you access the memory, the stronger it becomes and the longer it lasts.

Two types of long term memory exist. One is the declarative memory or explicit memory and the other is the non-declarative memory or implicit memory. The declarative memory involves the memories or information which are available in the conscious mode. It largely includes information that are facts, data, events and general knowledge, i.e. things that are known by many people.

Declarative memory is used many times in a day, if not throughout the day. For instance, remembering the time of an appointment or the time your children's school closes each day is a declarative memory. Learning how to ride a bicycle or a car is also a declarative memory. It can be easily recalled.

Declarative memory is divided into two parts: the semantic memory and the episodic memory. Semantic memory stores factual information, ideas, meaning and concepts, which are not dependent on personal experience. It is more about the knowledge of the world. There are many examples of semantic memory and to make you understand it, here is a list of some of them:

1. The knowledge that fishes win in water

2. The knowledge of the usefulness of a broom

3. The knowledge of the names of colors

4. The knowledge of what a pencil is used for

5. Knowledge of what a laptop is used for

6. Knowledge of the sun, moon and stars and what they look like.

7. Understanding of basic arithmetic like addition and multiplication

There are so many others. You will notice that the memories mentioned above are things that are generally known. Others include capitals of popular countries, languages, types of food and so on.

Episodic memory, on the other hand, involves memories that have to do with personal experiences and very specific events that happened in the past. It is the counterpart of the semantic memory.

This type of memory is usually unique such that if two people had the same experience, their recollection of the experience will be different. To form an episodic memory, your brain has to go through a process called encoding. The next step is consolidation, whereby the information is transferred permanently into the long term memory. The last step is the recollection process whereby the information pertaining to an incident is retrieved. There are many examples of episodic memory. Some of them are:

1. The movie you saw on your first date;

2. Your first day at a new job;

3. The day of your graduation;

Take for example your graduation day. Your remembrance of that day as the celebrant is going to be different from the remembrance of those who attended it.

There is another type of memory which is based on the combination of both the episodic memory and the semantic memory i.e. the combination of the personal experiences and general knowledge about the world. This memory is called the autobiographical memory.

Autobiographical memory is divided into four:

1. Personal memory: this is the type of memory that pertains to you only. Examples include your name, where you were born, the day, month or year you were born, and so on;

2. Reconstruction memory: this includes the rebuilding of the memories of an experience you once had, whereby the whole of your senses were active. The counterpart of this is the copies memory, which is a vivid memory of an experience you once had;

3. Specific memory: here, you have the memory of an event that happened a long time ago. The counterpart of this is the generic memory, whereby the memory of the event is not very detailed but kind of blurry;

4. Field memory is the type of memory which you can recollect in the original perspective, from the first person point of view. Its counterpart is the observer memory, which is from the third person point of view.

The autobiographical memory has three functions. One of the functions is the directive function whereby past experiences are used to solve present problems and also serve as a directive for the future. For instance, a man who was present at the birth of his first child many years ago will know what to do during the birth of his second child if he was present.

Another function of the autobiographical memory is the social function whereby social bonds are developed and maintained for people to have things to talk about. Intimacy and a stronger relationship bond can be forged among people when they share and talk about their personal experiences of events that happened in the past.

Another function is the self-representative function whereby personal experiences are used for the creation and maintenance of one's self-identity this can help with self-insight, self-worth and self-growth.

The last function is the adaptive function where past personal experiences can be used to maintain pleasurable or happy mood or even otherwise. For instance, you might be in a sad situation and in order not to feel depressed; you could use you past happy memory to override the sad situation and remain cheerful.

Another type of memory is the spatial memory, which is responsible for storing information that has to do with one's environment. For instance, to move around your city or town, you need the spatial memory to help you navigate the lay of the land.

The other type of the long term memory, the implicit or non-declarative memory is the unconscious or automatic memory. It uses the experience of the events that happened in the past to remember things without thinking about them. One type of implicit memory is the procedural memory which helps us to do many activities of everyday life without giving it any thought. It is the memory of how we do things.

To know the examples of procedural memory, think about the things you do unconsciously or automatically, without thinking about it. Examples are swimming, riding a bicycle, driving a car, using a pen, eating, playing football, playing the guitar, dialling a phone and so on.

Another type of implicit memory is the priming memory which involves using colors, pictures or words to remember or recognize both living things and non-living things. For instance, what do you think about when you hear the word red? You conjure up either an apple or blood, green for grass, blue for the sky and so on.

CHAPTER 3
RESEARCHES AND FINDINGS ABOUT THE MEMORY

Now that you know about the types of memory and how they function let's talk about some findings about the memory that you may never know before. Did you know that researchers have found out that when you remember some memories, it may cause some other memories to be forgotten? This means that sometimes, the things you decide to remember may be the cause of the things you forget.

Another finding is that when you access a memory that you once accessed, that memory can be changed. This is due to some activities going on in the brain which has to do with the neurons that pass the information back and forth.

Another finding is that a short nap can lead to a five-fold improvement in the memory. This is why sleeping helps the brain to boost faster. It serves as a form of refresh option. Sleeping helps the brain to rest and before more effective when it is reactivated.

Another surprising finding is that when you take pictures with your phone, it might cause disruptions for your memory of those events. Researchers show that it might be harder to remember the events you capture in your phone.

Another finding is that moving your eyes side to side for a few seconds can improve your memory as a result of a communication between some certain parts of the brain. This is especially useful information for students who wants to sit for an examination and have to do some memorizations.

WHY DO WE FORGET THINGS?

We have explored the memory and the types of memory. Some questions arise in the form that since our brains have a large memory capacity, why then does it become hard to retrieve the information stored in it? Why do we find it hard to remember events that happened in our past? Why do we forget things? Forgetting things can cause a lot of both personal and interpersonal problems like forgetting the birthday of your wife, husband, children or parents. It can be embarrasing and can even be frustrating. Many students can remember the number of times they forgot the answer to questions they already know in the examination hall. Imagine forgetting the password to your phone or laptop. There are many reasons why we forget things and we shall explore them.

One of the reasons is interference, a situation whereby some memories interfere with other memories. This is likely to happen when the memories are similar.

Interference can be proactive, a situation whereby an old memory makes it hard to remember a new one. It can also be retroactive, a situation whereby new information interferes with your ability to remember information you have previously learned.

Another reason is the failure to store crucial information. Distractions could cause this. An example is a student who was busy chatting with someone else on the phone and didn't really take in what the teacher was saying. When the exam comes, how can such a student remember? Or a husband who was busy watching his favourite sports channel and pretends to listen to what his wife was saying. That failure to store information can lead to serious problems.

Sometimes people also forget things deliberately. Perhaps, they were involved in a traumatic, depressing or embarrassing situation, such that remembering those situations could lead to depression. It is preferable to suppress such events voluntarily and deliberately.

It is also easy to forget things when you are doing too many things at the same time. Why trying to do many things at the same time, the brain will focus on one single thing and the others will be forgotten until it is too late.

Another reason is a phenomenon called memory decay. It means the information has already been stored; however, you are unable to retrieve it. This could be because you don't access that memory regularly and as a result, it may fade away. This is common among students sitting for an examination.

CHAPTER 4

MNEMONICS

Before we talk about the different ways of improving your memory, let's talk about mnemonics. Simply defined, mnemonics are memory devices or techniques that helps to retain information and aid retrieval of the information in the human memory. There are many examples of mnemonics.

In the late sixties, a scientist did a study and found out that students who used mnemonics had a higher percentage of test scores than those who don't. One of the examples of mnemonics is the **MEMORY PALACE.**

A memory palace is a virtual place in your mind where you can store information. With a memory palace, which takes time and practice, forgetting can become a thing of the past. There are many steps to create your own memory palace.

The first step is to imagine a palace. You can use the house you live in or a building you know so well. After that, create a route based on the order of the things you wish to remember and then decide on the way to travel through that route. Identify the locations of the memory you have stored.

For instance, let's say you used your house as your memory palace. Your living room could be where you store the memory of the date of birth of your wife; your kitchen could be where you saved the memory of your first date, and so on. When you have known all these, then you need to memorize the memory palace so that navigation will be easy. Use your creativity and use symbols to identify other memories.

Another example of mnemonics is the music mnemonic. This is very useful to students. With music, you can easily remember formulas, long lists and so on that could be asked in exam questions. Name mnemonic is another example where you used the name of a person, thing, animal or even country to remember the items in a long list

Word mnemonic is also an example, and here the first letter of a long list of items can be arranged to form a word. It is very common. For science students, they can use this technique to remember many of the scientific laws in science subjects like Chemistry and Physics.

Other types of mnemonic include the model mnemonic where you construct a representation or illustration of important information. Another is the rhyme mnemonic where you put the information in the form of a poem. In image mnemonic, you conjure up an image that helps you easily recollect the memory whenever you need it.

Connection mnemonic involves connecting the information you wish to remember to another knowledge you already have.

FIGHTING FORGETFULNESS

Several ways and strategies can be used to combat forgetfulness to prevent those embarrassments and frustrations.

Since it has been mentioned earlier that doing many things at the same time could lead to forgetfulness, it is therefore prudent to stop multitasking and perform a task one at a time and remember a lot of things after completing the task.

Another to fight forgetfulness is to repeat what someone says back to them. Some people might think it is not a smart thing to do, but it actually is. Also, try to be organized all the time and try to understand and notice the minute details.

CHAPTER 5

IMPROVING YOUR MEMORY: REMEMBER EVERYTHING AND ANYTHING

There are many ways to remember anything and everything. Mnemonics have already been mentioned in one way. Another way to remember anything and everything is to be interested in what you are learning. This is applicable to students. We are all students since we are always learning. When you become interested in learning, you become committed to it and when you are committed to it, you will always remember it.

However, if you find it boring, your brain will become lazy in making it memory, and then it eventually fades away.

Another way to improve your memory is to associate what you are trying to learn with the knowledge you already have. Also, writing down the information over and over helps you store it permanently in your memory such that when you pick up your pen, your hand sends signals to your brain, which in turn retrieves the information and then you begin to remember.

Summarization also helps the memory. In a situation whereby you have a lengthy note, you can summarize them into a shorter note which will help you conjure up the larger note for easy access.

Give your brain an exercise in the sense that you solve problems that are not familiar and with a lot of mental effort. The more exercises you give your brain to do, the better processing and retrieval of information you will be able to do. There are many advantages to this. One is that it is rewarding. As you continue to work out you brain, you become interested and experience more benefits and enjoyments.

The benefits of brain exercises include faster thinking and reaction time, self-confidence, sharp vision and hearing, less stress, good memory, positive mood improvement, enhanced creativity, extra motivation and productivity a mong others.

Also, you have the chance to learn something new and when you learn something new, you add more knowledge to your memory library or store.

Some of the examples of brain exercises include eating with chopsticks. This is very wise especially if you are the type of person that has always used spoons and forks to eat. Try using chopsticks and your brain will try to adjust to this new and challenging technique.

Another example is doing household chores with your eyes closed, doing things upside down or backwards, reading books aloud, simultaneously using all your senses, switching hands, doing things the hard way, taking a new hobby, meditating and so on.

Still, more examples are listening to the radio, dancing, crossword puzzles, storytelling, calculations, playing musical instruments, learning a new language and so on.

Do physical exercises which help the brain to remain sharp and active. There are many advantages of exercise to the brain. It boots the flow of oxygen to the brain; it reduces disorders that could lead to memory loss. There are also some brain chemicals in the brain that are very helpful, and these chemicals are enhanced by exercises.

Some physical exercises which improve the brain include outdoor exercises like the morning run, which keeps the body and the mind fit. For better results, it is best to do a training schedule, use the right clothes and eat a balanced diet that contains all the right nutrition. Morning runs also improve the memory.

Another exercise is cycling. To cycle, you need to pump both legs and the nerves in both legs send constant information to and fro the brain, thereby keeping the brain very active.

Yoga is another exercise that improves the brain. With yoga, you can improve your memory by having blood flow increasingly to the brain and it prevents the shrinking of the brain that may disturb the memory.

Another form of exercise is push-ups which help with umping blood to the brain and increased ability of the brain to learn through increased rate of reaction and coordination.

Jump rope exercises help to stimulate the brain improves body movement. It helps concentration improvement and attention. The brain function can also be improved by walking. It helps with brain repair, boosts the learning of motor skills, reduces stress, increases brain power and lowers stress levels.

Creating a regular sleeping schedule is another way to boost the brain. People who sleep less are less likely to remember things compared to people who have enough sleep. Sleep makes the brain rest and is essential and critical for memory consolidation and learning.

Sleep is very much necessary for cognition and sleep deprivation affects both attention and decision making. People who are sleep-deprived are less likely to be creative when compared to people who enjoy enough sleep because sleeping promotes creativity.

CHAPTER 6

THE UNLIMITED POTENTIAL

OF THE BRAIN

As mentioned earlier, the brain is a wonderful organ with astonishing functions. The brain consist of 100 billion cells and about 100,000 billion connections and despite this fact, no one has been able to use their brain's full potential. In order to use the full potential, you need to understand everything about what the brain can do. The brain is capable of doing a lot of things but it takes you to decide what you want to use it for.

With the memory palace and the ability to store and retrieve a lot of information, you can easily unlock the full potential of your brain. Since humans created supercomputers which can do very fast and complex jobs, it stands to reason that the human brain is far superior and can do more than that.

FOODS THAT IMPROVE THE BRAIN FUNCTION

There are so many foods that can help to boost the brain function and boost memory. These foods provide energy and help to protect the brain from diseases.

1. Green leafy vegetables: these help to prevent mental deterioration

2. Salmon: this helps to keep the brain running smoothly and improve memory.

3. Walnuts: this contains vitamin E which helps to improve cognitive health

4. Avocados: they contain vitamin K and help to prevent blood clots in the brain and also help to improve both the memory and concentration.

Other foods include egg yolk, beets, blueberries, bone broth, broccoli, celery and so on. With all these foods and the different techniques of boosting both the brain functions and the keeping and retrieval of memory, it is very easy to improve your memory to reach its unlimited potential.

CONCLUSION

Thank you again for buying this book!

I hope this book was able to help you understand the strategies needed to boost your memory and remember all the things you wish to remember anytime and anywhere.

The next step is to put all the strategies into practice and you become a human-super computer who can assimilate, understand anything, store them in your memory and retrieve them easily.

Finally, if you enjoyed this book, then I'd like to ask you for a favour; would you be kind enough to leave a review for this book? It'd be greatly appreciated!

Thank you and good luck!

www.ingramcontent.com/pod-product-compliance
Lightning Source LLC
Chambersburg PA
CBHW070950180426
43194CB00041B/2029